REAL JUSTICE:

BRANDED A
BABY KILLER

• • •

THE STORY OF TAMMY MARQUARDT

JASMINE D'COSTA

LORIMER

JAMES LORIMER & COMPANY LTD., PUBLISHERS
TORONTO

James Lorimer & Company Ltd., Publishers acknowledges the support of the
Ontario Arts Council. We acknowledge the support of the Canada Council for the
Arts which last year invested $24.3 million in writing and publishing throughout
Canada. We acknowledge the Government of Ontario through the Ontario Media
Development Corporation's Ontario Book Initiative.

Cover image: AIDWYC

Library and Archives Canada Cataloguing in Publication

D'Costa, Jasmine Anita Yvette, author
        Real justice: branded a baby killer : the story of Tammy Marquardt / Jasmine
D'Costa.

(Real justice)
Includes bibliographical references and index.
Issued in print and electronic formats.
ISBN 978-1-4594-0994-1 (bound).--ISBN 978-1-4594-0993-4 (pbk).--
ISBN 978-1-4594-0995-8 (epub)

        1. Marquardt, Tammy--Juvenile literature. 2. Smith, Charles Randal--
Juvenile literature. 3. Mother and infant--Ontario--Juvenile literature.
4. Trials (Infanticide)--Ontario--Whitby--Juvenile literature. 5. Judicial
error--Ontario--Whitby--Juvenile literature. I. Title. II. Series: Real justice
(Toronto, Ont.)
HV6541.C32D36 2015   j364.152'3092   C2015-903545-7
                                                   C2015-903546-5

James Lorimer &	Canadian edition	American edition
Company Ltd., Publishers	(978-1-4594-0993-4)	(978-1-4594-0994-1)
117 Peter St., Suite 304	distributed by:	distributed by:
Toronto, ON, Canada	Formac Lorimer Books	Lerner Publishing Group
M5V 2G9	5502 Atlantic Street	1251 Washington Ave N
www.lorimer.ca	Halifax, NS, Canada	Minneapolis, MN, USA
	B3H 1G4	55401

Printed and bound in Canada.
Manufactured by Friesens Corporation in Altona, Manitoba, Canada in May 2016.
Job #222753

In memory of my father, Gregory Joseph D'Costa, who taught me the spiritual injustice of even thinking with suspicion without absolute proof and who gave me a very strong sense of justice.

"Justice should be viewable under the micro-
scope, not from a telescope. And for that it
needs to be based not on law but on truth."

— Vera Nazarian,
The Perpetual Calendar of Inspiration

CONTENTS

1

CHAPTER ONE

A MOTHER CALLS FOR HELP

OCTOBER 9, 1993, 4:38 P.M.

The operator taking the 911 call tried to calm the panic-stricken woman on the other end of the wire.

"Police, fire, ambulance?"

"Ambulance."

"Stay on the line. I am connecting you with ambulance."

"Come on Kenneth, come . . ."

"You have to calm down now."

"He's not b-breathing." Her voice held the panic and fear that anyone holding a still baby would feel. But because she was the baby's mother, her terror was multiplied many times over.

"You have to calm down now," repeated the emergency operator.

"He's not breathing."

"Just calm down," she soothed.

"Oh my god!"

"Ambulance for which town?"

"Oshawa," Tammy replied, and went on to give the address.

"Okay," the operator said, "just settle down. Is that a house?"

"Yes. He's not b-b-breathing."

"We'll go in the front door," the calm voice said over the line.

"Side door. He's not *breathing* . . ." Her quivering voice had now risen to an hysterical pitch.

"Who's not breathing?"

"My son," the distraught mother said in agony. Tammy Marquardt looked at her two-and-a-half-year-old son cradled in her arms and sobbed into the phone.

"Ma'am, give him *CPR*. Do you understand what I'm asking?"

"I can't give him CPR. I can't, I don't know how, I've forgotten."

"Calm down and listen to my instructions."

Tammy could not listen. Her thoughts were running wildly all over the place. Her helpless baby . . . What if she blew into his lungs and they exploded?

"I can't, I can't . . ." she repeated.

Five minutes later, the ambulance was at her door.

★   ★   ★

Tammy Wynne was born in Ontario. Her father was an Ojibwa-Cree First Nations man and her mother was of European descent. Tammy was raised by her single mother. They lived in a basement apartment and then moved to a public housing complex on Lawrence Avenue East in Toronto.

Life was a struggle with poverty for Tammy and her mother. As a young teen, Tammy was pretty, with fresh looks and an inner excitement that made her glow as she set out to explore life and love. She was a mere wisp of a girl, not very tall, a slender reed that could be blown away by a strong wind.

Her trials began when her mother's boyfriend started to make sexual advances towards her. She had to escape this. So in 1989, when she was barely seventeen, she left home. Most girls her age were in high school. They lived at home with their families, and had the protection of their parents. Tammy was outside the safety net that most kids take for granted. She had to fend for herself. She lived in shelters and at friends' homes when they would have her. Tammy struggled to make it through high school. Happiness seemed like an event, rather than a condition. A Christmas visit to family did not make up for the isolation and struggles that made her vulnerable.

However, Tammy was young and resilient. She had some good moments. She was excited as she posed in front of the mirror, dressed up to go to her high school dance. What she saw pleased her. Her brown eyes sparkled, her short, silken auburn hair framed her face, and the red dress she had borrowed made her feel like a princess. She never imagined in that moment that her future would be so painful.

When Tammy met Robert Nelson, she hooked up with him. At eighteen, she got pregnant with Robert's child. This caused her to leave school in April 1991. She had not yet finished grade 12. Kenneth Wynne was born on May 18, 1991. Tammy, now nineteen, looked at this miracle in her arms. Though she was barely ready to look after a child, she already loved him. Sadly, her relationship with Robert did not last. Tammy was alone again. She was still young and needed nurturing. She needed someone to watch out for her and her child. But she lacked a support system. She was living at a home for single mothers when she reconnected with Rick Marquardt, a former boyfriend. Tammy and Rick married in March 1993. They moved into an apartment together on Lloyd Street in Oshawa, Ontario.

★   ★   ★

October 9 started like any other day. Tammy woke up at 7:30 a.m. with Kenneth. She sat him down to breakfast, gave him some Cheerios, and turned on the cartoons. Around 8:00 a.m., Rick received a call from his ex-girlfriend, Jeannine. He put down the phone and looked at Tammy.

"What did she want?" Tammy asked.

"She's in labour and ready to give birth. She wants me to go out there and be with her."

"Well?"

"I don't have money right now," he said, looking at her hopefully.

Tammy wordlessly gave him her bank card. Rick left to help Jeannine at the hospital. The weather forecast called for rain that day, so Tammy decided to stay indoors with Kenneth. She spent the rest of the morning at home with him, watching cartoons and playing. In the afternoon, mother and son decided to take a siesta. Tammy moved Kenneth to the spare bed in her room.

The two of them napped for a couple of hours.

She woke up around 4:00 p.m. and went to the washroom. When she was there, she heard Kenneth call, "Mommy, Mommy." Tammy strained her ears. The voice seemed muffled.

"Mommy's in the washroom. I will be there soon." She finished up and went to attend to her son. She found Kenneth rolled up in the bedding. His head was at the foot of the bed, and he was twisted in the sheets down to his chest. He was so tangled up in the sheets that she found it hard to get him out. She started to panic.

"Mommy, Mommy," Kenneth repeated.

"Mommy's here, it's okay, Mommy's going to get you out."

Then his words dwindled to just a faint "Mom." At this point, Tammy knew that there was something very wrong. She thought of using scissors to cut him out of the tangle. However she worried she might cut him. This made her struggle with the sheets. She finally freed him from the bedding. By this time, Kenneth had turned white and he did not seem to be breathing. She picked him up in her arms, ran to the phone, and dialled 911.

2

CHAPTER TWO

A MOTHER LOSES HER SON

"THERE'S NO TRAGEDY IN LIFE LIKE THE
DEATH OF A CHILD. THINGS NEVER GET BACK
TO THE WAY THEY WERE."

— DWIGHT D. EISENHOWER,
AMERICAN PRESIDENT

Tammy placed the baby on the couch. She opened the door for the paramedics and showed them to where Kenneth lay still. His face had turned ash grey and he was not breathing. Kenneth had "lost all visible signs of life," as court documents would later describe. Tammy clutched the coat sleeve of the paramedic in fear.

"Please make him breathe," she pleaded.

"Calm down," the paramedic said.

As they tried to revive the still child, Tammy kept talking, "He is just out of the Oshawa General after breaking his leg . . . he has a history of *epilepsy* . . . make him breathe . . ."

It is hard to imagine the intense fear she felt: the fear of losing her child.

The efforts of the paramedics to revive Kenneth at the apartment failed. They took him to Oshawa General Hospital. Tammy rode in the front of the ambulance. Her heart was in her mouth. Soon after Kenneth's admission, an emergency physician attended to him. The toddler was having a heart attack. Ten minutes later, Kenneth's heart began to beat once again. It seemed like a lifetime to Tammy. The doctor placed him on a ventilator. This is a machine that moves air in and out of the lungs to help him breathe normally. The doctor faced Tammy, who was breathless since she arrived.

"We have to transfer Kenneth to Sick Kids in Toronto."

At 7:12 p.m. that evening, Kenneth went by ambulance to Sick Kids Hospital. There was no room for Tammy to go with him.

This was the start of the next phase of Tammy's nightmare. As if from nowhere, police appeared. They offered to give Tammy a ride in their cruiser. Tammy was frantic to get to Sick Kids and be with her child who was dying. Grateful for the ride, she went with them. However, instead of taking her to the hospital, they took her to the police station. What happened next was a blur of questions. Tammy reported the details later in her statement in court.

"What happened? Where were you?" asked an officer.

Her head was spinning and her brain was yelling at her. *Stop. Kenneth is dying. I have to get there.*

The police went on. "Was there anyone else there?"

At this point, her husband, Rick, arrived at the police station.

The police looked at him briefly. They turned back and continued the probing. "Did anyone call? Did anyone visit?"

Tammy put her hands to her ears to make it go away. *Stop, stop, don't you understand my child is dying? Don't you have kids?* All these thoughts were racing in her head. She answered their questions as best as she could under stress.

"Were you by yourself?" continued the officer.

The police were relentless. The questions kept coming and Tammy's answers were videotaped. All she wanted was to get to her son. Finally, she was taken to Sick Kids Hospital to be with Kenneth. Looking back, it was not routine for the police to separate her from her son in such a crisis.

At Sick Kids, Dr. Shemie, a *paediatric* intensive care

specialist, examined Kenneth.

"He is in a deep coma with minimal brain function. My diagnosis is that Kenneth has a severe brain injury caused by a lack of oxygen."

Tammy did not know what that would mean for her child. From his practice, Dr. Shemie knew that Kenneth could not be saved. He sat Tammy down and explained the matter to her. He urged her to donate Kenneth's liver, kidneys, and heart. He said that it would help to save other children in need. Tammy agreed to the donation.

Three days later, Kenneth was declared brain dead. It was Tuesday, October 12, 1993. They took off the machines that had kept him going. Kenneth was pronounced dead. The stated cause of death was a lack of oxygen and blood flow to his brain.

Tammy was numbed by the events. She was unsure of what to feel. No child should die before his or her parents. But death is not foreseen. We all know we will die someday. However, we are never really prepared for it.

Was this the death of an otherwise healthy child? This would be the key question as the drama unfolded. It would also be the basis on which Tammy would finally be acquitted.

Kenneth had several health problems in his very young life. He suffered from asthma. This is a chronic disease. It

causes shortness of breath, tightness in the chest, cough-
ing, and wheezing. Kenneth's asthma made him more
vulnerable to other kinds of illnesses. In January 1992, he
got pneumonia. This causes swelling of the lungs.

As if that were not enough, Kenneth also had epilepsy.
This is a brain disorder that causes seizures. Sometimes
they occur along with fits of tremors. Tammy also suffered from epilepsy. Even so, she found Kenneth's attacks
terrifying. He would shake and thrash his legs and make
gurgling sounds. This would last several minutes. Once it
lasted as long as eight minutes. Tammy had taken Kenneth
to Sick Kids several times because of his seizures. Twice,
he had to be taken by ambulance. The pills to stop the
seizures didn't seem to help. Kenneth's last hospital visit
had been in September 1993, just a month before his
death.

Through his sickness, Tammy did what any mother
would do. She tried to get him the help he needed.

Dr. Shemie was at a loss. Tammy gave him Kenneth's
medical history. He was not convinced that Kenneth's
death was due to his past history. He did not believe that
he had all the facts. He was suspicious of Tammy's story.

So much affects our judgment of others. Our views
are based on all kinds of things. Most of all, they are
based on our experiences. But sometimes, prejudice gets

in the way. Little voices in our head ask questions. Can someone poor, from a different culture, or, perhaps a teen mother, love their children or take care of them as well as "regular people"? At this point, Dr. Shemie chose to play it safe. He called in the SCAN (Suspected Child Abuse and Neglect) Program. It links Sick Kids to community agencies, doctors, hospitals, children's aid societies, police, and schools.

Tammy had just lost her baby boy. She didn't think her life could get any worse. She was wrong.

3

CHAPTER THREE

CAN A POOR TEEN MOM LOVE HER
CHILD?

"A MOTHER'S BODY REMEMBERS HER BABIES —
THE FOLDS OF SOFT FLESH, THE SOFTLY
FURRED SCALP AGAINST HER NOSE. EACH CHILD
HAS ITS OWN ENTREATIES TO BODY AND SOUL."
— BARBARA KINGSOLVER

OCTOBER 21, 1993

The wind had dropped and the temperatures had cooled down greatly. It was just a couple of weeks after Kenneth had died. Tammy was slowly waking to the reality that she could never hold her son in her arms again. She felt restless. The apartment seemed tiny. Her thoughts and memories of Kenneth were everywhere. She needed to get out.

Tammy went to a bar with her husband, Rick, and

two of his friends, Stewart Powell and Stacey Craig. She was feeling numb with grief. But quite another feeling crept upon her like a cancer. It was guilt. The guilt of being a mother who survived when her baby had died. It began to eat at her. She felt sick to her stomach. As she sat in the bar with the other three, she tried to drown the feeling with drink. The feeling would not go away. She vomited. It was a tortured woman within her who screamed repeatedly, "I forgot how to do CPR. I could have saved him. I killed Kenneth. If I remembered how . . . I am to blame. I killed him. I could have saved him if I had remembered how to give him CPR."

Rick tried to calm her down.

"I want to go to the cemetery," she cried.

The four friends got up and left the bar. They drove Tammy to the cemetery. Tammy stood by the grave of her son and broke down. She shouted, and her voice echoed in the quiet night and stillness of the graveyard. "I killed him. I forgot how to give CPR. Oh god! I killed him."

Killed him, killed him, killed him echoed back in her ears, like the dead had come alive to haunt her. She ran towards the road to shut out the words. The others tried to stop her from running on the road but Tammy tried several times to throw herself in front of passing traffic. She kept shouting, "I killed him. I forgot how to give

CPR. It's all my fault." Then, as she tried again to throw herself in front of a car, Powell punched her. She fell down and struck her head on the pavement.

They took her to the Scarborough General Hospital. The hospital was worried that Tammy might try to hurt herself again. They tried to admit her but Rick acted quickly. He spirited the now-quiet Tammy out of the hospital and took her home.

The hospital reported the missing patient to the police. Shortly after, the police showed up at her home. This set Tammy off once again. She got hysterical in front of the police. Every action of hers worked against her. She had raised their suspicions.

Tammy should have been allowed to grieve. Instead, the authorities believed that Kenneth had been murdered. Tammy was their prime suspect.

★   ★   ★

Parenting is not easy. It is even harder with a chronically sick child. Tammy had asked for help from the system before Kenneth was born, as well as during his brief life. Most first-time mothers, above all, teen moms, need help and guidance from family and friends. Tammy had no such help. During her pregnancy she lived at Rosalie Hall, a maternity home for pregnant teens. After giving birth, she spent time with them to get support and counselling.

Maureen Edwards, her social worker, visited her at her home after she gave birth. Tammy was struggling with the huge task of caring for baby Kenneth. "I have occasional blackouts, and Kenneth is difficult to soothe. Sometimes when I feed him and burp him, I imagine that I am putting my arms around his neck. Sometimes, when I can't soothe him, I yell at him," she confided.

Maureen Edwards heard Tammy's fears. She advised her on how to handle Kenneth when he was fussy. In another instance, Tammy told Cathy Sorichetti, another social worker who visited her, "Kenneth kept crying, and I placed my hand over his mouth to stop."

Cathy did not believe Kenneth was in danger. She knew it was hard for a teen to cope with raising a child on her own. She suggested, "Perhaps it would be a good idea if you put Kenneth in care."

"Oh no," Tammy responded, "I am his mother. I am just afraid that I may accidentally hurt him if I fall asleep while feeding and burping him."

Tammy had only expressed her fears that fatigue might affect her parenting. The social workers misread Tammy's words. When they testified in court later, they created a different impression of the young mother.

Her youth and her lack of family support for raising a sick child created a huge challenge. Tammy suffered bouts of depression as a result. She also turned to drugs to cope. She badly needed a break. On January 25, 1993, she visited the office of Frances Holmes, a Toronto *Children's Aid Society (CAS)* worker. It was the same year that Kenneth died. She asked that Kenneth be placed in a foster home. She explained, "I live in a basement apartment with Kenneth and two other adults. My living conditions are cramped. My husband is being physically abusive to me. I am stressed and worried I might hurt Kenneth."

The next day, Frances Holmes visited her home. Tammy once again asked for Kenneth to be put in the care of CAS. The CAS issued a three-month custody order and placed Kenneth in foster care. Kenneth returned home after the three months.

On July 5, 1993, Tammy moved to the Oshawa YMCA to get away from Rick Marquardt. Their marriage was stormy. She needed time alone.

A week later, she told Marlene Wikaruk, a supervisor at the YMCA, that she had squeezed Kenneth's leg, causing a bruise. Marlene did not ask to see the bruise. She warned Tammy, "I will have to report this."

Tammy offered no protest. Marlene was impressed that Tammy had volunteered to tell her this. She had no worries after spending some time with Tammy. She viewed this as a cry for help. Tammy returned home to her husband.

September 9, 1993 was a windy and rainy day. The Marquardt family decided to stay home. Kenneth and Rick were playing on the back porch when Kenneth fell and broke his leg. Tammy took Kenneth to Oshawa General Hospital. He was kept there for a month. She visited her young son every day at the hospital. He was discharged on October 6, 1993.

All these events worked against Tammy. Tammy was an easy target. She was seen by the system as a poor, young mother with low parenting and coping skills. She was also in an unstable relationship with her husband. But was she a murderer?

As the investigation unfolded, Tammy became the only suspect. The authorities suggested that she had smothered her son in a moment of frustration. A post-mortem was done on Kenneth's body. *Pathologist* Dr. Charles Smith was the director of the Ontario Paediatric Forensic Pathology Unit at Sick Kids. Dr. Smith concluded in his report that Kenneth's death was caused by *asphyxia*, through smothering or strangulation.

On November 23, 1993, Tammy Marquardt was charged with the murder of her son, Kenneth. She was later released on bail pending her trial.

While Tammy waited for her case to come up for trial, she became pregnant. Tammy was getting another chance to be a mother. On August 17, 1994, Tammy gave birth to Keith. This was the baby she had talked to, sung to, and grown to love over the nine months that she had carried him. He felt like a miracle. He was her second chance, a part of her. But as soon as she gave birth, the CAS took Keith away from her. There seemed no end to the pain Tammy had to endure. It was like losing a limb or some deep vital organ from inside her body. But above all, a child had lost his mother. Tammy was permitted to visit him once a week.

As the trial date approached in 1995, Keith's father, Rick Marquardt, disappeared from her life. Tammy became pregnant for the third time. The father was a man she dated briefly after Rick left.

Tammy worried about what would happen at the trial. She also worried about what would happen to the child she carried. She couldn't bear to lose another baby.

CHAPTER FOUR

THE TRIAL OF TAMMY MARQUARDT

In the fall of 1995, Tammy's case came up for trial. Before the trial, the *Crown prosecutor* offered Tammy a five-year plea bargain. They wanted Tammy to plead guilty. In exchange, her prison sentence would be a reduced term of five years. The evening before the trial, the two lawyers representing her visited with her. They did not agree on her odds.

"There is not enough proof here to get you convicted," one lawyer told her.

"The Crown's offering you a plea of *manslaughter* for five years — take it!" argued the second lawyer.

Tammy sat there, dismayed. She was firm with her lawyers.

"I haven't done anything. Why should I take it?"

Tammy insisted that she was innocent. She turned down the offer of a reduced sentence of five years. She would not plead guilty to manslaughter. The case went to trial the next day.

"Please rise."

With these words ringing through the courtroom, Tammy's trial began. She was charged with the murder of her two-and-a-half-year-old son.

The case came before Justice McIssac and a *jury* in Whitby, Ontario. The normal process is that once a jury is selected, the defence lawyer is allowed to question the jurors. This is to ensure that they don't hold strong opinions (called a *bias*) on the case before actually hearing the evidence. Jurors have to make their decision based only on what they hear in court.

Tammy's lawyer asked the first juror, "Do you have a bias against claims of child-killing?"

The judge stopped him. He felt that the charge of baby-killing would likely stir deep feelings in most people. But he also felt that strong feelings do not equal an unfair bias. The judge felt the jurors' feelings would not affect their *verdict* in this case. The judge stopped the lawyer's line of questioning. So, the jurors did not go through the normal process of review. Any bias against Tammy was not revealed. Thus began the trial.

The Crown prosecutor went over all the details of how Tammy found Kenneth tangled in his sheets. Then

Tammy's lawyer read from Tammy's sworn statement of fact. She described finding Kenneth:

> *When the police later asked me how long this all took, I said about twenty minutes . . . that is how long it seemed to me. For some reason, I noticed the clock in the bedroom said 4:33 . . . so my time estimate was off. I can only say it seemed like an eternity as I tried to extricate Kenneth from the sheets.*

He read on: "Kenneth was white and he did not seem to be breathing. I ran with him in my arms to the phone and called 911."

Then it came to light that she had failed to give CPR. The prosecutor asked her, "Why not?"

"Because I could hardly breathe myself."

"What do you mean, you could hardly breathe yourself?"

"I was crying a lot and really upset."

The prosecutor's case hinged on two main theories. The first one focused on Tammy's lifestyle. She was financially and emotionally strained. She was young and lacked the coping skills needed to raise a small child, especially one with health problems. Tammy's marriage was unstable. Her husband was abusive. The prosecutor tried to show how a stressed-out Tammy could easily "lose it" and strangle her child.

The second theory was based on the opinion of the expert Dr. Charles Smith. Dr. Smith believed that Kenneth had been smothered. He did not think his death was caused by a seizure.

Tammy sat through the trial with a sinking heart. It was very hard to hear her character being ripped and slashed over and over again. The Crown focused on Tammy's actions and behaviour, her *demeanour*, to portray her as a potential killer.

Society often judges a person based on their outward appearance or their actions. But we all express our feelings differently. For example, some people cry when they are sad; others seem calm. No one can know for sure what another person is feeling or thinking simply by looking at them.

The Crown called a series of witnesses. They had all dealt with Tammy before and after Kenneth was born. What ensued were, in Tammy's heart and mind, several acts of betrayal.

5

CHAPTER FIVE

TAMMY'S DEMEANOUR IS QUESTIONED

"CHOOSE YOUR COMPANY BEFORE YOU CHOOSE
YOUR DRINK."

— GAELIC PROVERB

How should a mother whose son is dying behave? How should she look later as she buries him? Why didn't Tammy act the way others thought she should? Did her actions amount to a display of guilt?

The Crown called many witnesses. They were asked to describe how Tammy behaved after Kenneth's crisis. Some very different versions emerged.

The Crown first called upon Tony Romano. He was the first paramedic to arrive on the scene:

"How would you describe Ms. Marquardt's manner when you arrived at her home?"

"I found her distraught and really emotional."

Various staff from the Oshawa General Hospital were questioned next:

"Dr. Muhra, how would you describe her manner during the time that Kenneth was at the hospital?"

"I would say she was clearly upset," the doctor replied.

When Nurse Harding took the stand, she said: "I found her to be very calm and offhand . . ."

When Police Constable Terry took the stand, the Crown asked: "How can you describe her manner?"

"She was hysterical and anxious at the Oshawa General Hospital," the constable replied.

Police Constable Kluem also testified. He said, "She was very emotionally upset. She came across as a timid person."

Then the Crown questioned those at the Sick Kids in Toronto. The nurses' viewpoints seemed to differ. It was a long time between Tammy's visit to the police station and her arrival at Sick Kids. Perhaps, she had the time to calm herself. Perhaps she was just too tired to show any feelings. But the witnesses were merciless. It seemed like they had already condemned her. Nurse Haley had taken hospital notes that had described Tammy as "very emotional." However, when she was on the stand, she said, "She did not seem overly upset. It seemed like she was just saying the words. But her body language didn't match it."

Nurse Haley's *testimony* did not match her original notes. This went unquestioned.

Next up was Nurse Page. "I found Tammy to be happy at Kenneth's bedside at Sick Kids," she said.

Dr. Huyer took the stand. He stated, "She laughed at an [inappropriate] and macabre comment I made." This should have been a mark against Dr. Huyer, rather than Tammy.

Next, the Crown called Sergeant Naccarato to the stand. He had talked to Tammy at the hospital. "She wasn't too upset," he said.

Detective Carroll, who arrested Tammy on November 23, 1993, was called to the stand. After her arrest, the detective interviewed Tammy. He explained the charge of murder to her. When he outlined his theory that Tammy killed Kenneth out of frustration ". . . She just gave me a glaring stare. That was her [manner] for the full time that I was with her."

Tammy sat there feeling helpless. She was only twenty-one. She looked like a mere child herself. Her hope was draining away. She grieved the loss of her child. She feared the loss of her freedom. She felt betrayed by those she had confided to in her weak moments. *Tammy this . . . and Tammy that . . .* She listened in a blur, feeling totally numb.

But there was more to come. The Crown called Stewart Powell and Stacey Craig to the stand. Their evidence rang little bells of doubt in the minds of the jury.

On the night of October 21, 1993, Tammy had gone out to the bar with Rick, Stewart, and Stacey. She got very drunk. She had hoped to escape her despair. Her outbursts about the anguish and guilt she felt came up at the trial. At the bar, her behaviour seemed understandable. She was a mother grieving the loss of a son. At the trial, it took on a completely different hue.

The prosecutor called Stewart Powell to the stand. Powell recounted the events of that evening. Then he added, "She looked me directly in the eye and admitted that she had killed Kenneth."

"In your opinion, was she expressing her guilt in the sense of an intentional killing or merely expressing guilt over not being able to do CPR?" the Crown prosecutor asked.

"I would say intentional killing."

Stacey Craig was called to the stand. She also confirmed that Tammy had meant she had killed her son Kenneth on purpose.

Tammy responded in her own defence. "Yes, I screamed, 'It's all my fault. I killed Kenneth. I forgot how to do CPR. It's all my fault.' It sounds disgusting. I wanted to dig Kenneth up and drop myself in to where he was. I wanted to die. I wanted to be with him."

Friends and family also testified about her manner at the funeral. Tammy's estranged sister took the stand. She said, "She only cried during the service but treated the funeral like a party."

Stewart Powell had also testified, "She was joking around at the funeral."

Again, Tammy replied on her own behalf. "I was numb," she said.

As the trial went on, it was clear that the witnesses had very different views on Tammy's behaviour.

The prosecutor had tried to prove Tammy's guilt based on her lifestyle. Next, he tried to prove that Kenneth did not die from epilepsy.

CHAPTER SIX

THE DAMNING TESTIMONY OF DR.
CHARLES SMITH

"THERE IS NOTHING WORSE THAN A POMPOUS
EXPERT."
— JUSTICE HASKELL M. PITLUCK

Enter Dr. Charles Smith. He was a slender man. He looked wan and wore glasses. He didn't look like a man who would end up ruining so many innocent lives. At the time of Kenneth's death, he was the rock star of *pathology*. His job was to examine a dead body and find out what caused the death. At this time, his work focused on children. It was his evidence that robbed Tammy of her freedom.

When he was called to the stand, he introduced himself. He said with an air of grandeur, "I am Dr. Charles Smith, director of the Ontario Paediatric Forensic Pathology Unit. This unit is the only one of its kind in the world. I have probably done more paediatric *forensic* work than anyone else in Canada and have performed more than 1,000 child autopsies in my career."

It was not just a harmless boast. It seemed like a dare to anyone who would question his judgment.

Dr. Smith had conducted Kenneth's *autopsy*.

"And in your opinion, what was the cause of death of Kenneth?" asked the Crown prosecutor.

"In my opinion, the cause of death in this case was asphyxia, which causes irreversible brain damage."

"Could you explain to the court the term asphyxia?"

Dr. Smith said that asphyxia is a lack of oxygen in the blood. Oxygen is vital to the body and all its organs. If the body lacks oxygen in any way, it will cause damage.

The Crown prosecutor then brought out snapshots. They were photos of Kenneth taken after he died. He gave them to Dr. Smith. The doctor pointed to tiny red spots on Kenneth's skin. "These are caused by bleeding," explained Dr. Smith. The Crown prosecutor took the photographs and showed them to the jury.

Dr. Smith went on. He gave an example of how these marks could happen. "I would say that these [spots] we see suggest asphyxia. I did not find any external injury. But I found some tiny red spots in the lower part of Kenneth's neck."

"Is it possible that there could be another reason as to how Kenneth got those marks?" the Crown prosecutor inquired.

"It is possible that it could have been caused by the paramedics when they were giving CPR," he admitted to the court. "Kenneth's brain was extremely swollen."

The Crown prosecutor walked over to the jury. He showed them snaps of Kenneth's skull and of his brain. Tammy's little body cringed. They were speaking of her son in such a cold way. She wanted to remember the child she had held in her arms, clever and laughing. But she was facing a grave danger now. All she could do was numb herself to get rid of the pain.

At this point, Dr. Smith gave a possible cause of how Kenneth's oxygen had stopped: ". . . [It] could be caused by something like a plastic bag or [smothering]. It could be a neck compression," Dr. Smith went on.

This strengthened the prosecutor's case. Tammy sat frozen, shocked.

"Dr. Smith, how long would you say it would take to cause a child's heart to stop beating through [smothering]?"

"I would say, between ten and twenty minutes."

"Are the findings that you made on Kenneth Wynne's body consistent with [smothering] with a soft object?"

"Yes, they are."

"And are they also consistent with [smothering] with a plastic bag or some such other object?"

"Yes, they are."

"Is there anything else that your findings are consistent with?"

"It's possible that someone held his nose and mouth closed. Maybe he was [smothered] that way."

The prosecutor then walked up to the jury and addressed Dr. Charles Smith.

"Could this be caused by an epileptic seizure?"

"I can't accept that . . . unless you have other evidence to support it. I don't . . . if someone with the knowledge of seizures in kids comes along and disagrees with me, then I could be convinced . . . such a person is obviously better informed than I am."

Tammy's petite body slumped in her chair. *This is an unreal dream . . . no, a nightmare.* She looked blank. She did not know what to feel. She was numbed by the loss of her child and self-blame for not remembering how to give CPR. But deep within her, a slow anger burned. The doctor's testimony fueled her anger. She knew he was wrong. She was the only one who knew the truth.

Dr. Charles Smith was still on the stand. He spoke on: "I did not see any signs of a seizure disorder when I did the autopsy. I do recognize that there is a problem of sudden death that can occur with epilepsy . . . but unless the person drowns or inhales their own vomit, there would not be evidence of asphyxia."

"Could you comment on Ms. Marquardt's statements that Kenneth called out 'Mommy, Mommy' before he went lifeless?"

"If that's true, then the seizure theory cannot be used to explain Kenneth's death. But, if a child neurologist tells you something else, then please believe him or her."

Then the Crown asked if Kenneth's death could have been caused by disease. Dr. Smith responded, "No, I rather wish [it] could have . . ."

Dr. Smith's role was to help get to the truth of what had happened that day. But he had used the witness stand to aid the prosecutor's theory of murder. The jury listened intently to Dr. Smith's opinions. He was considered the expert, after all. The situation did not look good for Tammy. Her only hope rested on the doctors who had treated Kenneth for epilepsy.

CHAPTER SEVEN

DID KENNETH DIE FROM EPILEPSY?

"IF IT WERE NOT FOR HOPES, THE HEART
WOULD BREAK."

— THOMAS FULLER

Tammy felt her freedom slowly slipping away from her. The full shock of her situation had yet to come. But she held on to a faint light of hope. She hoped that Kenneth's doctors would provide proof of her innocence. She held her hands in her lap as if in prayer.

The Crown prosecutor called in Dr. Caspin, Kenneth's family doctor.

"Dr. Caspin, can you inform the court on Kenneth's medical condition?"

"I only know of three seizures that Kenneth had in the first twenty months of his life. However, they were all linked to when he was feverish. Hence it held no weight.

I know that Kenneth was on anti-seizure drugs. But the Sick Kids was following Kenneth's seizure disorder, not myself."

Next, Dr. Miroslav Ort, a child specialist in private practice, was called to the stand. He was asked to describe the little boy's health.

"Kenneth's first meeting with me was on July 6, 1993. His mother, Tammy, had brought him in. She said that he had suffered seven seizures. She said that he also had fever during two of these seizures and became unconscious. He became stiff. He had jerky movements of his hands and feet. I was concerned by what she told me. So I ordered a brain scan."

Kenneth suffered another seizure on the very night of his first visit to Dr. Ort. Tammy took him to Oshawa General Hospital.

Dr. Ort continued, "Tammy thought that Kenneth had a fever that night at the Oshawa General Hospital. But the chart with details of his admission had no record of fever. I had changed his drugs because of the after-effects of those he was taking at that time. But I put him on an anti-seizure drug, Dilantin. This is a basic drug for epilepsy. Kenneth took this drug until his death."

Tammy tried to listen to the witnesses. The statements about Kenneth's health were vital to her defense. She had to prove that Kenneth may have died from epilepsy that sometimes caused sudden death.

Dr. Shemie, a children's doctor at Sick Kids, was called to the stand. He had tested Kenneth's blood. He found that there was not enough anti-seizure drugs in Kenneth's blood to stop him from having a seizure.

Dr. William Logan, a child *neurologist* and the chief neurologist at Sick Kids, was called upon next. He had treated Kenneth when he arrived by ambulance on October 9, 1993. He explained to the court, "For young kids, a seizure with fever is a common, fairly mild condition. Epileptic seizures, however, resulting from a brain abnormality, can result in death."

Tammy's hope brightened at this point. Perhaps the jury would see her innocence. She held her breath. But as Dr. Logan continued with his evidence, her heart sank.

"The data I had was that he had had a previous history of seizures. But most of these were linked to fever or caused by fever. One of them . . . was not linked with fever."

Tammy looked at the jury. How were they taking in this data? She could not tell. She could only hope. She leaned forward as if to listen clearly.

Dr. Logan spoke on: "His growth and health otherwise was fine except for asthma. The event that was stated as preceding his loss of consciousness was unusual."

The Crown prosecutor then questioned Dr. Logan. "Do you believe that, in this case, Kenneth was having a seizure prior to the state of being wrapped up in the sheets?"

"He may or may not have been having a seizure at that time. It didn't quite explain it totally in my mind. Though there are cases of sudden death in epilepsy."

"Dr. Logan, is sudden death in epilepsy an explanation in Kenneth's case?"

"No."

"Dr. Logan, can a person speak during an epileptic seizure?"

"If they do, they might be having a mild seizure. However, in most cases, they wouldn't be speaking or making sense."

"Would that involve a loss of consciousness?"

"Not while they are speaking. It could lead to that later. Once unconscious, a person suffering a seizure might still make sounds."

Despite her past of being abused, losing her child, and finding herself in this difficulty, Tammy stood up to defend herself. She was the sole witness for her defence. Tammy took the stand and told her story over and over again. She was always constant with all the facts. She had found Kenneth tangled in the sheets. She was afraid to give CPR. She called 911.

The jury heard her evidence. "I felt responsible for his death. I told myself if I had not gone to sleep, if I had not gone to the bathroom, if I had got to the bedroom sooner, if I had got the sheets off him sooner, if I could only have remembered how to do CPR properly, he would not have died."

She stepped down. She now sat clutching her fists in her lap, waiting for the closing.

In her heart, she held fast to the hope that surely the jury would see she was innocent.

She hoped that her new baby would not be born in prison.

8

CHAPTER EIGHT

TAMMY IS CONVICTED

"RATHER LET THE CRIME OF THE GUILTY GO
UNPUNISHED THAN CONDEMN THE INNOCENT."
— JUSTINIAN I

It was October 24, 1995. The case of the Crown versus
Tammy was closing.

In her closing speech, the prosecutor asked the jury
to rule that Tammy had smothered Kenneth.

> *Her worries and frustrations, her insecurities,
> whatever her feelings . . . came to a head at
> that point . . . She went to Kenneth's room and
> her feelings translated into action . . . Kenneth
> Wynne died at her hand. The seizures were just
> a 'red herring' . . . Dr. Smith in his evidence
> did not accept that a seizure caused Kenneth's*

> *death . . . that if there had been no obstruction*
> *to his breath, his death from seizure was even*
> *less likely . . . all the doctors have agreed that for*
> *there to be any air of reality to this theory . . .*
> *there has to be something more than that.*

The prosecutor was compelling. The jury listened closely. Tammy sat there unsure. Where could this lead? She held on to that one thing she had left. Hope.

The prosecutor went on:

> *. . . [Dr. Smith's] conclusions, as with all the*
> *other doctors . . . is worth very, very serious con-*
> *sideration. In fact . . . there is no evidence before*
> *you to contradict any of the opinions of the doc-*
> *tors. I therefore urge you to conclude that Tammy*
> *Marquardt suffocated Kenneth to death.*

Tammy's lawyer had no medical proof to give the jury. He rose to make his closing speech, "Kenneth's death may indeed have been caused by a seizure."

Tammy sat up in her chair. Perhaps her lawyer would win. Maybe there was still hope.

He went on:

The doctors were intent on looking at one thing . . . I'm not suggesting for a moment that Dr. Smith and Dr. Logan, most importantly Dr. Smith, wasn't doing his job the way he would do on each and every occasion. Very experienced and very, very eminent medical practitioner . . . I'm just asking, was the alternative that we suggest ever considered by the doctors? No one looked carefully at his history . . . not because they were being negligent . . . not because they were being incompetent . . . but . . . because it was a stone, that wasn't turned over is what I'm suggesting . . . The seizures are not fanciful . . . I fully recognize the collective weight of the medical opinion. It suggests that Kenneth was not in a post-seizure state when he died . . . and if that can be determined by an autopsy, then so be it. But I submit . . . that it is not a completely clear conclusion.

The judge then charged the jury to consider all the facts in the case.

"The Crown has a single theory that Tammy [smothered] Kenneth in some way. The medical proof the Crown offered was from several well qualified doctors. While all agree that he had died from asphyxia, there is nothing exact in their proof to a death by [smothering]. The best they could do is state that Kenneth's death suggests such a process. Nothing was found in the care of the deceased from October 9 and following to suggest that seizure formed any part of the cause of the asphyxia."

The judge then reminded the jury to consider two other points. First, the doctors couldn't be certain that Kenneth didn't have a seizure that day. Second, the doctors could not say for sure that Kenneth didn't have epilepsy.

★   ★   ★

It was October 24, 1995, the day of a full eclipse of the sun. The jury returned with their verdict. Silence filled the courtroom. Tammy stood before the judge. All she heard was "Guilty," and her sun blacked out. Tammy was convicted of second-degree murder in the death of her son Kenneth.

On December 7, 1995, Tammy was sentenced to life imprisonment without eligibility for *parole* for ten years. It was the start of the eclipse of her freedom for fourteen long years.

9

CHAPTER NINE

A MOTHER LOSES HER SON — A SON
LOSES HIS MOTHER

"WHAT LIGHT IS TO THE EYES — WHAT AIR
IS TO THE LUNGS — WHAT LOVE IS TO THE
HEART, LIBERTY IS TO THE SOUL OF MAN."
                    — ROBERT GREEN INGERSOLL

Tammy was convicted of a crime she did not do. At the time of the trial, she was out on bail. She had to live under strict rules at Rosalie Hall in Toronto. It was a home for single mothers in trouble. On October 24, 1995, the day she was convicted, her bail was cancelled. She was taken to the Whitby jail.

Up to the day she was convicted, Tammy was allowed to visit her fourteen-month-old son, Keith. Her visits with him were controlled. Her *conviction* changed that, too. Keith was put in foster care. Tammy did not see or hear from Keith in all the years she spent in jail.

Once she was sentenced to life imprisonment, Tammy was moved from jail to the Prison for Women, in Kingston, Ontario. She stared at the imposing structure that was to be her new home. Her freedom was gone but there was worse to come. She put her hand on her tummy as if to reassure the child inside her. She was alone, yet she was not. She felt the new life stirring.

One of the guards in the prison offered her advice. She knew how the inmates thought and how they acted by their own code.

"If you want that child inside of you to live, you'd better lie and say you killed your husband."

Even amongst prisoners, there is a pecking order to crimes. The inmates graded child killers as the lowest of the low. Though Tammy took the guard's advice, she could not keep up the lie for long. Her case came up on a television news program. This made the inmates more hostile towards her. Tammy had to watch her back. Her third son, Eric, was born on June 20, 1996, at the Kingston General Hospital. He was whisked away from her arms within twenty-four hours. He lost his mother. Tammy lost yet another child.

Eric was made a Crown ward, just like Keith had been made two years before.

Tammy was a wreck. It was not just her mind. The normal physical discomfort following childbirth was worse without her baby to nurse or cuddle. It heightened the utter despair she felt from losing her children. It deepened her outrage from losing her freedom over a *murder that never was.*

Tammy was taken back to the Prison for Women in Kingston. Eric was brought to her off and on. He was then put up for adoption.

"Please let Eric and Keith be adopted by the same family. I want them to grow up as brothers together," she pleaded to the authorities.

They honoured her wishes. Keith and Eric lived together with their adopted family. They did not see their mother again.

The authorities allowed Tammy to write a letter to Keith and Eric. It was to be opened when they turned eighteen. She later told reporters, "The only way I can describe the feeling of it is to have your heart ripped out . . . and have someone hold it in front of you, basically, until it stops beating. The pain is so deep that there are no words."

Tammy suffered alone in prison. She was innocent but nobody believed her. Then a fellow inmate decided to make Tammy's life even worse.

10

CHAPTER TEN

TAMMY'S LIFE IN PRISON

"THE HUMAN BODY HAS LIMITATIONS. THE
HUMAN SPIRIT IS BOUNDLESS."
— DEAN KARNAZES

Tammy's life in jail was fraught with risks. She was bullied by other inmates. They taunted and threatened her. All because they believed she had killed her child.

One morning, a woman I will refer to as Ms. X walked past Tammy's cell and spat at her. Tammy was a new mother, getting over the death of her son Kenneth and the loss of two other sons. She saw the blob of spit on the floor. She wondered if the other inmates were guilty of the crimes they were accused of. She wondered about a couple of inmates in the cells near her. They were banging their heads against the bars. Were they doing it because they were innocent? Had they reached the end of their endurance? She did not want to end up like that. She had to do something to prevent her own decline. A week later, Ms. X walked past Tammy's cell and threw feces at her. It hit the bars and splayed to the floor. A couple of days later, Ms. X threw urine between the bars.

There is an old game called broken telephone. You whisper something into the ear of the person next to you. Then they pass the message to the next person, and so on. Along the way, the message gets very distorted. Rumours about Tammy went around the jail. The story got worse as it was passed on. They said that Tammy had "nuked her kid." Others said she had "put him in a roasting pan and ate him for Thanksgiving dinner."

To protect Tammy, the guards blocked access to her cell. All of Tammy's five senses were alert to her surroundings. Her ears echoed with the sounds of screams, insults, and heads banging against bars. Her nose was assaulted with the stink flung at her. Her eyes witnessed sorrow, despair, and suicide. Her tongue longed for the taste of good food — *oh, for a steak!* And she so wanted to touch her sons. Maybe prisoners had to pay a price to society for their crime . . . but she was innocent.

Tammy was offered counselling. Throughout her ordeal she maintained that she was innocent. But the professionals who tried to help her believed she was guilty. It was hard to move past this barrier between them.

★   ★   ★

In the spring of 1997, Tammy was transferred to the Grand Valley Institution in Kitchener, Ontario. This was a new kind of prison that had just opened that year. It was modelled on the concept of a village. It had ten slope-roofed cottages. Each could house eight inmates. The cottages were bounded by a grass lawn. Each had a public living room, dining room, porch, and kitchen. It also had a private laundry, study, and bathroom.

Earlier prisons held a ring of cells around a central security and watch-out booth. This prison enclosed a multi-use chapel. The corridors were bright. Quiet colours gave it a feel of normal living. The grounds had a pleasant landscape. Tammy entered it still hoping she would be found innocent and sent home.

The Grand Valley prison offered several programs to help the inmates. Tammy knew that she needed to be a model prisoner in order to get parole or *appeal* her case. She took part in as many programs as possible. She did courses in anger and emotion management. Anger seemed the only companion that was keeping her from despair. She also took substance-abuse treatment. Through all this, she received many good reports from her program leaders.

Although her life had been full of sorrow, Tammy still had hopes for a future. She was about to meet hurdles that challenged her very desire to live.

11

CHAPTER ELEVEN

TAMMY APPEALS HER CONVICTION

"AWFUL LONELINESS OF SPIRIT IS THE
ULTIMATE TRAGEDY OF LIFE. WHEN YOU'VE
GOT TO THAT, REALLY REACHED IT, WITHOUT
HOPE, WITHOUT ESCAPE, YOU DIE. YOU JUST
CAN'T BEAR IT, AND YOU DIE."
— ELIZABETH VON ARNIM, *IN THE MOUNTAINS*

Tammy spent three years in jail hoping to appeal her conviction. She hoped to find justice, be found innocent, and be free again.

For five days in January 1998, Ontario faced one of the fiercest ice storms in its history. The result was $5.5 billion in losses. Tammy's life at the time was very like the ice storm. But her loss could not be measured.

Tammy appealed her conviction in court on January 16, 1998. She was not successful. The main reason was that there was no new evidence to consider in the case. Without new proof, there was no reason to believe she was not guilty.

Tammy then learned that the adoption of her sons Keith and Eric was finalized. She realized she had lost her sons completely. Their new parents did not want them to have any contact with their birth mother. The hope that had been her companion through her prison life vanished. She had reached the end of the road.

For the next six months, Tammy dragged her anguished body through her prison chores. A voice in her head kept repeating, *There is nothing to live for, nothing to live for.* So, in July 1998, she finally gave up. She took a large quantity of pills and tried to end her life.

Tammy lay quite close to death. The prison officials rushed her to St. Mary's General Hospital in Kitchener. The hospital immediately took action. They pumped her stomach and revived her. She spent three days in recovery. She was then transferred once again to the Prison for Women in Kingston.

Now she was not just imprisoned by society, but also by her body, which had been forced to live. Prison life had taken away every choice she had. She could not look at the sky when she wanted. She couldn't eat what she wanted or choose what to do. She had to bathe when told and wear what was given to her. And now, the final choice had been taken away. She had to live without wanting to.

She spent the next two years in Kingston. The Archambault Commission, which examined the penitentiary system in Canada, called the Prison for Women "unfit for bears, let alone women." Finally, public outcry caused the prison to close down in 2000.

Tammy was moved back to Grand Valley prison for the rest of her sentence. She endured verbal abuse and threats of physical harm from other inmates. She was alone. She had no support from family or friends. Above all, she had no hope. At this low point, she reached for help. The Native Sisterhood, a support group of native women in the jail, helped her get back on track. She learned that she was never truly alone. She also learned that she could cope with the pain in her life.

Tammy made a decision to stay alive and get out of jail. Her goal was to see her sons again. Someday she would find them. She would tell them her story.

In October 2000, Dr. Nexhipi did a psychological review of Tammy. She firmly refused to admit that she had killed Kenneth. She maintained her innocence. Dr. Nexhipi recommended that Tammy read Dr. Smith's report that said Kenneth died from being smothered.

In every way, Dr. Smith's opinion affected her life. Even in jail, her doctors used the report as the basis of their reviews. Dr. Nexhipi wrote that Tammy had amnesia, built to block out her past, as well as what "she had done" to Kenneth.

Once again, Tammy took all the courses the prison offered. In 2001, Tammy's efforts began to pay off. She was granted brief visits to the local epilepsy society. It seemed apt. Both Tammy and Kenneth had seizures in the past. She was considered a minimum security risk now. The visits were training her to take part in the outside world.

Tammy was nearing the time for her parole hearing. Parole is the early release of an inmate. When a prisoner is let out on parole, they have to live under very strict rules. If they break the rules, they are sent back to prison.

In March 2004, the parole board let Tammy begin a special year-long program. During this time, she lived in jail but was allowed controlled visits to the Elizabeth Fry Society in Toronto. Amongst other things, the society helps women prisoners. Soon, Tammy became a leader with the Alternatives to Violence program at Grand Valley prison. She was slowly picking up the threads of her life. Being in jail had narrowed her choices, but she was making the best of what she had. Though the wait was endless, there seemed to be a light at the end of the tunnel.

Also in 2004, Tammy met a new lawyer, John Hill. John advised Tammy to seek the help of the *Association in Defence of the Wrongly Convicted (AIDWYC)* in Toronto. She met them, and they assigned David Bayliss to her case. Shortly before her parole was granted, David met with her in jail. He told her that AIDWYC would study her case. If their review was good, they would adopt her defence. It was the start of her return to justice. AIDWYC was to play a vital part in proving Tammy's innocence. She was still not sure whether they would find a way to clear her, but it brought her some hope. Her spirits lifted.

In June 2005, she got her first free day pass to go to the Elizabeth Fry Society in Toronto. At last, after spending ten years locked up Tammy was granted day parole. During her parole, they let her live in a halfway house run by the Elizabeth Fry Society in Toronto. Day parole meant that during the day, Tammy could join in area activities to get her ready for full parole. She had to return to the halfway house each night.

Finding a job is never easy. Everyone finds it hard, but it is harder with a criminal record. Breaking into the job market with no skills was tough. Tammy had to compete for low-skilled jobs with youth and students. Tammy was not a kid any more. She was now in her early thirties. She could find only short-term jobs. She worked at a cafe at

Canada's Wonderland, then at a bookstore, and later at a plant in Toronto.

She had to live in a world that she had left ten years back. So many things had changed. For instance, she was new to cellphones and Internet. She found it hard to fit into society outside the prison walls. Tammy's life on the outside was not as she had hoped. She stopped taking her pills for depression. The calendar was nearing the date of Kenneth's death. It was not the right time for her to stop her pills. She began to get more and more depressed. As the date drew nearer, she was tortured with thoughts of Kenneth's death. She lacked sleep and had nightmares. She had to make them go away. She tried the only way she knew — drugs and alcohol. This was against the rules of parole. In the fall of 2006, Tammy was sent back to prison when she tested positive for cocaine.

She had slipped. She could not bear to think that her little Kenneth was dead. Mothers take care of their kids, protect them. But she had not been able to do that for Kenneth. But worse than that despair was that she had been wrongly accused of killing him.

Although she was granted parole again a few weeks later, it was reversed in April 2007, when she was again caught with cocaine. A month later, she was out but it did not last. Tammy couldn't adjust to life in the outside world.

She ended up back in prison on November 30, 2007.

But all was not lost. In the background of all Tammy's troubles with her life on the outside, a very different pot was stirring in Toronto.

Tammy's grade 2 class picture from St. Margaret's Public School, Toronto in 1979–1980. Tammy is on the far right in the first row.
Margaret Wynne.

This is Tammy's grade 2 picture from St. Margaret's Public School in Toronto, 1979. Margaret Wynne.

Tammy is pictured here in her backyard in 1980, age 8.
Margaret Wynne.

Seventeen-year-old Tammy appears to be looking forward to life as she poses in front of the Christmas tree in 1989.
Margaret Wynne.

Tammy, 18, and her sister Carol, 22, are balancing on Santa's knee in this December 1990 photo. Santa is their Uncle Tom. Photos don't always reflect internal struggles and unhappiness.
Margaret Wynne.

The door to a typical cell inside Kingston's Prison for Women where Tammy was held. Willy Vestering.

A hallway inside Kingston's Prison for Women. Willy Vestering.

Tammy was in Kingston's Prison for Women on Halloween in 1996. Here she is dressed as a devil.
Margaret Wynne.

In 2001, Tammy got the approval to have temporary absences from Grand Valley Institution to the local epilepsy society. Her security classification was changed from medium to minimum. Margaret Wynne.

Tammy and AIDWYC lawyer, James Lockyer, celebrate her appeal victory in February 2011. AIDWYC.

Tammy is surrounded by the media in February 2011 just after the charge of murder was quashed and a new trial was ordered. AIDWYC.

Tammy, holding a picture of her son Kenneth, was given her freedom on June 7, 2011. The court acknowledged that she was a victim of a miscarriage of justice. AIDWYC.

Tammy received $250,000 plus the cost of her legal fees from the Ontario government because of her wrongful conviction. All those who were wrongfully convicted because of Dr. Charles Smith's testimony and inaccurate findings received the same amount. AIDWYC.

12

CHAPTER TWELVE

THE RISE AND FALL OF DR. CHARLES SMITH

"IT IS WRONG ALWAYS, EVERYWHERE, AND FOR ANYONE, TO BELIEVE ANYTHING UPON IN-SUFFICIENT EVIDENCE."

— WILLIAM KINGDON CLIFFORD, *THE ETHICS OF BELIEF AND OTHER ESSAYS*

Charles Smith was born in a Toronto Salvation Army hospital. Three months later, his mother put him up for adoption. His new father served in the Canadian Forces. They moved often. First they moved around Canada and then to Germany. The young Charles went to high school in Ottawa. He finished medical school at the University of Saskatchewan in 1975. He spent many years looking for his birth mother. At last, on her sixty-fifth birthday he found her. He called her, but she refused to talk to him.

In 1979, Dr. Charles Smith worked in surgery for a year at Sick Kids. He then moved on to pathology training and specialized in working with children. After his training at Sick Kids, Dr. Smith began doing child autopsies in 1981. He started with kids who had died of accidental and natural causes. During the next ten years, Dr. Smith began to oversee cases that involved crimes (known as forensic pathology). Although he should have got extra training for this work, he didn't. Training for this kind of work did not exist in Canada at that time. It was brought in later, in 2008. Dr. Smith soon became the most experienced doctor in the country in this field.

Despite his lack of training, Sick Kids and the *Office of the Chief Coroner for Ontario (OCCO)* appointed him director of the *Ontario Paediatric Forensic Pathology Unit (OPFPU)* in 1992. The OPFPU did autopsies on most of the kids who died in and around Toronto. He was not chosen because of his skill. He was the only pathologist who wanted the job.

At the time, Dr. Smith didn't think his lack of training was a problem. However, later he confessed, "My forensic pathology training was woefully inadequate."

Over the course of the 1990s, Dr. Smith acquired star status in his field. His practice seemed to be unequalled. He became the go-to expert for all the complex and suspicious child deaths. In many of these cases, his view on the cause of death was considered fact. He strongly swayed the outcome of any case. So, when Tammy's case was heard, Dr. Charles Smith took centre stage in both the trial and the verdict. Nobody challenged his expert opinion.

Dr. Smith's private life influenced his work. Many of the victims of his flawed evidence were young, single moms. He was a member of the Christian and Missionary Alliance of Canada. Dr. Smith told the media, "I have been fuelled by my life's purpose — finding out the truth for parents who have lost babies."

Sadly for Tammy, she lost her babies, her freedom, and her youth in large part due to the evidence of Dr. Charles Smith. Tammy's journey to prove her innocence was in a strange way tied into the death of a child named Amber, in Timmins, Ontario.

In the summer of 1988, twelve-year-old SM (name under publication ban) was hired to babysit Amber three days a week. Amber's parents checked SM's background. They felt they could trust her with their sixteen-month-old daughter. SM had taken the Red Cross babysitting course and was a good student. SM had great reviews from other parents.

On July 28, 1988, Amber woke from a nap. She wriggled out of SM's arms, and tumbled down the stairs. She struck her head in the fall which caused fatal brain damage. Amber died two days later at Sick Kids in Toronto. SM was charged with manslaughter based on the findings of Dr. Charles Smith. He changed the original report that said Amber had died from a fall. He told the police that Amber had died of *shaken baby syndrome.*

SM's father (DM) did not accept that his child had been charged with such a crime. He researched shaken baby syndrome. He was a chemist and used his skills in science and huge sums of money to fight for his daughter. DM found nineteen experts around the world with knowledge and studies that backed his child's innocence. He paid for nine experts to fly to Timmins for the trial. Written views from the other ten experts were produced in court. DM went bankrupt to cover the costs of SM's defence. But it was a landmark case. Not only was she *acquitted,* but it raised doubts about the work of Dr. Charles Smith.

Fingers pointed to his previous cases and questioned his method of working. Complaints poured in. His status took a hit. Dr. Smith began to be known for late cases. Samples went missing from his messy desk.

But Ontario's chief coroner, Dr. James Young, and his deputy, Dr. James Cairns, (Smith's bosses) refused to see his faults. This was partly because they also lacked any expert training in the field. Both men had played a big role in propping up Dr. Smith's career. Later, it came to light that they protected him from critics who had warned of his flaws as much as seventeen years ago.

Several cases where Dr. Charles Smith had given evidence were re-opened. The complaints against him were being reviewed. Dr. Smith was sliding down a very steep slope.

While all this was going on, Tammy was still in prison. AIDWYC was busy reviewing her case. Tammy felt a mix of hope and anger. She was edgy and this kept her blood flowing and her mind active. Tammy wanted freedom. She grieved the loss of the years. She should have spent them raising her two boys. These feelings only increased her anger. Her anger was aimed at one man, Dr. Charles Smith. She knew that the system had let her down. But Dr. Smith had played the most cruel and damning part of them all.

13

CHAPTER THIRTEEN

DR. SMITH'S CASES ARE REVIEWED

"MAN'S CAPACITY FOR JUSTICE MAKES
DEMOCRACY POSSIBLE, BUT MAN'S INCLINATION
TO INJUSTICE MAKES DEMOCRACY NECESSARY."
— REINHOLD NIEBUHR

In 2001, Dr. Charles Smith's boss resigned. On June 30, 2001, he was temporarily replaced by Deputy Chief Coroner Dr. Barry McLellan. Amongst other things, Dr. McLellan made some new rules. Dr. Charles Smith was not allowed to do any more autopsies in suspicious deaths.

The following year, the *College of Physicians and Surgeons of Ontario (CPSO)* upheld three complaints about Dr. Smith's earlier work. Dr. Smith was cautioned by the CPSO for being too rigid. They said his conclusions often overstated the facts.

In April 2005, AIDWYC wrote to Dr. McLellan and the attorney general of Ontario. They requested a full public review of Dr. Smith's work. By this time, the media had covered many cases in which Dr. Smith had played a key role in wrongful verdicts.

Two months later, Dr. McLellan announced a Chief Coroner's Review. It cited "concerns raised" about a number of cases where Dr. Smith was the main pathologist. On November 1, 2005, Dr. McLellan announced that forty-four of Dr. Charles Smith's cases would be reviewed. Four outside pathologists were picked to do the Review.

Dr. Smith resigned from Sick Kids in 2005, before the hearings began. His pay for 2004 was $290,000. During this time, Dr. Smith lived with his wife and two kids on a farm in Newmarket, Ontario. His marriage didn't last. He told the media, "My marriage was under pressure and ended due to the stress of the very publicized events."

As the Review unfolded, Kenneth's case was added to the list. This took it to a total of forty-five.

Dr. Pekka Saukko, a forensic pathologist from Finland, was asked to review Kenneth's case. Dr. Saukko looked at all the proof and medical reports. He filed his report on Kenneth's autopsy on December 14, 2006. He stated that there was not enough proof of asphyxia. He said: "The cause of death should be given as [unknown]."

He said that it was wrong to give any cause of death if all likely causes could not be ruled out. "In such a case, the death has to be classified accordingly as [unknown]."

Early in the Review, it became clear that Tammy's claim of innocence was true. But there were still so many hoops to jump through. Many actions had been set into motion. She had to wait.

Tammy looked at the sky, waiting to be free. She sometimes despaired that it would never really happen. She thought of her two boys. They were out there somewhere in the world with their new parents. What were they doing? Did they know about her? She made a new resolve to hold on to life. She would be free. She would find them. She would tell them her side of the story.

Flaws were being found in Dr. Smith's evidence in many cases. At last, Dr. McLellan released his Chief Coroner's Review on April 19, 2007. The review found that Smith had made mistakes in twenty cases in the deaths of kids. The review cast doubt on verdicts in thirteen of the cases.

"I am very surprised with the overall results of the review, and concerned," Dr. McLellan said. "In a number of cases, the reviewers felt that Dr. Smith had given a view about the cause of death that was not rightly backed by the evidence on hand for review."

The chief coroner shared the results with the lawyers involved in all of the concerned cases. The public began losing faith in the system. Six days after the release of the Review, the premier of Ontario, Dalton McGuinty, set up the *Inquiry into Paediatric Forensic Pathology in Ontario*. Justice Stephen T. Goudge was put in charge. He was asked to review the policies and practices in Ontario from 1981 to 2001. The purpose of the inquiry was to see what had gone wrong. He was to advise how to fix the failures. Most of Dr. Charles Smith's cases were put under study.

The Goudge inquiry was not designed to change wrongful verdicts. It could not fix the fact that Tammy had spent over ten years in prison. But it could help her appeal her conviction.

The Goudge inquiry asked Dr. Saukko to look into Kenneth's death. Dr. Saukko handed in his findings in October 2007. He appeared at the Goudge inquiry in 2008. According to Dr. Saukko, Dr. Smith's work on Kenneth's case and his autopsy were "deficient." He stated that Smith's version of the cause of death was "in error." He also said that the evidence that Smith presented at Tammy's preliminary inquiry and trial was "unprofessional" and "misleading."

Dr. Saukko's report was accepted in full. Four experts who reviewed the case confirmed Dr. Saukko's findings.

So did Dr. Michael Pollanen, the new chief forensic pathologist for Ontario. The Goudge inquiry found that Dr. Smith's lack of training was the main reason for his mistakes.

Case by case, the Goudge inquiry reviewed deaths where Dr. Smith had testified. James Lockyer from AIDWYC also appeared before the commission to speak on Tammy's behalf. AIDWYC accepts cases for defence only after doing their own probes. They take up cases only when they believe that a client was wrongly convicted. AIDWYC was convinced of Tammy's innocence.

★   ★   ★

Tammy needed new evidence to get an appeal. She resolved to build her case. Tammy hired her own expert. Through counsel, she found Dr. Simon Avis to review Kenneth's case.

Dr. Avis, the chief medical examiner for Newfoundland and Labrador, reviewed Kenneth's past of seizures. He concluded that Kenneth had epilepsy. There was no clear proof of the cause of death. The Dilantin levels (the drug to prevent seizures) in Kenneth's blood were too low to prevent seizures. All this showed that a seizure could have caused his death. He also found no proof of smothering.

The Crown hired its own expert, Dr. Christopher Milroy. Dr. Milroy agreed with Dr. Avis. He found that Kenneth's death could be given as "[unknown]." He advised,

"I agree that there is no proof of smothering. An expert in child neurology should check whether Kenneth had epilepsy . . . A child expert could also check whether Kenneth's manner as described by Tammy could happen with an epileptic seizure."

Tammy then took a big risk. She engaged Dr. Elizabeth Donner. Dr. Donner was known as the top expert in Canada on epilepsy in kids and sudden death in epilepsy. She was on staff at Sick Kids. Tammy was in jail because of the staff at Sick Kids. But Tammy believed in her own innocence.

Taking Dr. Milroy's advice, the Crown hired its own expert, Dr. Carter Snead, also from Sick Kids. Both doctors reviewed the cause of Kenneth's death.

Dr. Donner's expert opinion was that ". . . Kenneth had epilepsy." She noted that it was obvious enough for his doctors to prescribe an anti-seizure drug. Her finding challenged one of the Crown's main theories in Tammy's conviction. Dr. Snead agreed with Dr. Donner. She said that the cause of Kenneth's death could be *Sudden and Unexpected Death in Epilepsy (SUDEP)*.

The findings gave Tammy the new proof she needed to seek an appeal. But Tammy's deadline to apply was drawing near. She was in a race against the clock.

Tammy looked around her jail cell with a feeling of hope. *At last,* she thought, *I will be able to prove my innocence. At last I shall be free. At last, I can find my boys. I shall make them proud of me. They will never have to feel ashamed of their mother.*

14

CHAPTER FOURTEEN

TAMMY IS RELEASED ON BAIL

"IF YOU MAKE A MISTAKE AND DO NOT
CORRECT IT, THIS IS CALLED A MISTAKE."
— CONFUCIUS

All those involved in Tammy's conviction seemed to agree that a mistake had occurred. In 1998 she had tried to appeal her conviction but the appeal was denied. Now, on February 10, 2009, she applied to the Supreme Court of Canada to have that decision reversed. If it went well, she would be able to ask again for an appeal of her conviction.

On March 12, 2009, Tammy was brought to court. Her hands were shackled in front of her. She was escorted by guards from the Grand Valley prison.

Tammy looked around the crowded courtroom. She saw her high school law teacher, Michael Cyijetic. On the other side sat William Mullins-Johnson. He had spent twelve years in prison after being wrongly convicted of killing his four-year-old niece. He was another victim of the testimony of Dr. Charles Smith. She smiled at the sight of these friends who believed in her. She stepped into the prisoner's box.

Tammy's lawyer, James Lockyer, requested bail for his client. The Crown counsel, Gillian Roberts, agreed. The appeal court judge ordered that she be released on bail until the Supreme Court gave their decision. It was a moment of incredible joy for Tammy. The courtroom broke out into loud cheers.

March 2009, weather historians say, was the clearest month of the year. For Tammy, too, it seemed like she was closer to clearing her name. Her bail release was the first step in proving her innocence. As Tammy moved to the door, towards what she believed would be bright sunshine and warmth, James Lockyer stopped her.

"Do up your coat, Tammy, it's cold outside."

With that bit of advice from her lawyer, Tammy stepped out into the cold winter air. She took a deep breath. The sun was indeed shining bright. Cameras, microphones, and flashing lights stormed her at the exit. She had spent thirteen years and eight months in prison. She soaked in the feeling of freedom. Journalists pushed microphones in her direction. The questions rained on her. Tammy was too happy to answer them.

"How do you feel?"

"I feel totally amazing. This is my day. I'm out, I made it," she told them, as she stood outside Osgoode Hall. "I'm just overwhelmed and excited to finally have my freedom."

"What do you have to say to Dr. Charles Smith?"

"I just have one thing I want to say to him and that's 'Why?' I am also angry at the people that employed him. I just hope and pray that the system changes. I hope that through the Goudge inquiry, this won't happen to another person again, because ... I wouldn't wish this on my worst enemy. My experience was like a living hell."

"Are you in contact with your sons?"

"No. I would like to have contact with my two sons. They were taken away from me when they were barely a day old. They are now teenagers who live with an adopted family."

"Do you know where they are?"

"No. I don't even know if they know who I am. I just hope they know one day what happened. They are going to want to hear the truth. I am the only one who can give it to them. It is the thought of them that helped me get through prison life. I hope they are watching TV right now. I don't even know if they know who I am. When they are ready, they'll find me."

"Is there anything you look forward to? Like any food for instance?"

"Melba toast," she said. Then she turned to William Mullins-Johnson and embraced him. "Thank you for being here." She wiped away her tears. Tammy strolled away from the courthouse holding Mullins-Johnson's hand. Both, entwined in kinship — victims of the justice system and the evidence of Dr. Charles Smith.

Some of the media turned to Tammy's lawyer. James Lockyer, the co-founder of AIDWYC, offered,

> *We are waiting for the Supreme Court of Canada to give its decision on whether the case will be reopened. We have fresh evidence in several guises . . . Dr. Simon Avis, chief medical examiner of Newfoundland and Labrador has provided an opinion. It entirely discredits everything that Dr. Smith said back in 1995. It explains that pathology can no longer determine the cause of Kenneth's death . . . but there is every reason to believe he died as a result of seizures he suffered from all his life.*

Would her appeal be heard? While she waited for the answer, Tammy had to live in a Toronto treatment centre. She was managed by the Toronto Bail Program. Although Tammy was released by the court, she had no family support or money to pay for her bail. The Toronto Bail Program helped people like her. But she was not completely free. She had to live by the rules of the bail program.

She had spent nearly fourteen years away from normal living. It had deprived her of many life skills. She was out of her depth. She knew the truth was out there. Dr. Charles Smith had been discredited. But how long would it take to prove she was innocent? The wait was tough. She told reporters, "If they still had capital punishment, I would be dead. Thank god Canada doesn't have the death penalty anymore."

On April 30, 2009, the Supreme Court of Canada referred the case back to the Court of Appeal for Ontario. Tammy's appeal would be heard. The court was told to consider the fresh evidence of Dr. Avis and Dr. Donner. It also had to decide whether Tammy's conviction was due to a failure of the justice system.

Tammy spent six months in Grant House, a live-in healing centre. She then lived in Langley House, a post-healing, live-in centre, for a further five months. Later, she

15

CHAPTER FIFTEEN

DR. CHARLES SMITH IS REPRIMANDED

"WHENEVER A DOCTOR CANNOT DO GOOD, HE MUST BE KEPT FROM DOING HARM."

— HIPPOCRATES

On February 1, 2011, Dr. Charles Smith was brought before the Discipline Committee of the College of Physicians and Surgeons of Ontario (CPSO).

A Statement of Facts was filed before them. Briefly, the statement said that Dr. Smith showed a lack of knowledge, skill, and judgment. He behaved without honour, shame, or ethic. He made many mistakes when stating causes of death. His autopsy findings were often wrong. He let his personal *prejudice* against some parents influence his work.

Dr. Smith's counsel agreed with the findings. The committee found that Dr. Smith was guilty of professional misconduct. They described his practice as "disgraceful, dishonourable, or unprofessional." They declared him incompetent.

Dr. Smith lost his licence to practice medicine in Ontario. He was told to appear before a panel and told to pay costs of $3,650.00 within sixty days. Dr. Smith did not attend the public hearing about his failures. The panel read their statement anyway. It concluded on this note:

> *The medical profession strives to act morally, ethically, and with the best interests of our patients . . . we are sometimes called upon to serve the administration of justice in our courts. By your actions you abysmally failed to do so in these areas . . . and disgraced our profession. We publicly deplore and denounce your behaviour. Nothing we can do or say will repair the damage you have caused to the lives of the persons you have injured. What we can do is express . . . the abhorrence of the profession and the public for your misconduct.*

So many lives were ruined by Dr. Smith. $3,650.00 didn't seem like much for all the damage he did. While the sun set on Dr. Charles Smith's career that February, there was bright sunshine in Tammy's life.

On February 10, 2011, her case came before three judges. They listened to the arguments. They did not rely just on the Goudge inquiry report. They also heard the proof given by doctors Avis, Milroy, Donner, and Snead.

The appeal was a success. At the end of the hearing, the judges said:

> It is manifestly in the interests of justice that the fresh evidence be admitted on this appeal . . . the evidence demonstrates that the . . . conviction constitutes a miscarriage of justice . . . it is tragic that it has taken so long to uncover the flawed pathological evidence that so clearly contributed to the appellant's conviction in 1995.

Tammy's conviction for murder was set aside and a new trial was ordered. Tammy's lawyer told the court that he planned to seek an *acquittal* at the new trial. That would give her a "not guilty" verdict.

But Tammy didn't want to go through a new trial. She knew an acquittal would take a long time. She wasn't sure she could prove her innocence. She was anxious and edgy. The pressures on her were too much. She started taking drugs again. Her emotional state worsened. She could not bear the long wait, the doubt, and the haunting nightmares. So, instead of seeking an acquittal, Tammy agreed to simply have the charges withdrawn. James Lockyer arranged an early court date.

All was not over yet. But Tammy was getting closer to the end of her nightmares.

She told the media that day, "I'm just looking forward to having it over with. I try not to look back to my time in prison, but it's hard."

16

CHAPTER SIXTEEN

TAMMY'S FINAL DAY IN COURT

"STONE WALLS DO NOT A PRISON MAKE, NOR
IRON BARS A CAGE."

— RICHARD LOVELACE

It was a hot summer's day on June 7, 2011. Tammy appeared in court in a blue sleeveless dress. Her tattooed arm was exposed for all to see. In 1995, when she was first convicted, Tammy inscribed the word "freedom" on her arm. On this day, she sat in the court of Justice Michael Brown, waiting to hear that the charges against her would soon be withdrawn.

"Good morning."

Tammy's counsel, James Lockyer, stood up.

"Good morning, Your Honour."

So began Tammy's final day at court. Indeed, it was to be a good morning for Tammy.

Mr. Greg O'Driscoll, the Crown counsel, stood up. He exchanged the polite greetings with Justice Brown, and went on to explain, "This case is before the court as a result of the Court of Appeal setting aside the conviction for second-degree murder and ordering a new trial . . . For reasons which I will set out, the Crown . . . will not proceed with a new trial. I will ask that the charge against Ms. Marquardt be withdrawn."

He outlined to the judge the details of the case. He finished by saying that the new evidence changed the Crown's theory.

Tammy leaned forward with hope, tense, waiting to hear the words.

Mr. O'Driscoll admitted that Dr. Smith's testimony appeared to be flawed. It was possible that Kenneth died from SUDEP (Sudden and Unexpected Death in Epilepsy). In fact, cause of death was officially unknown.

There was silence in the court. Tammy was feeling the strain. The hearing seemed to be going on for a long time. They were close to the end.

"[I am asking that the charge against Ms. Marquardt be marked withdrawn by the Crown. Thank you, Your Honour.]"

Mr. Greg O'Driscoll took his seat. The judge turned to Tammy's counsel, James Lockyer.

"Thank you very much, Mr. O'Driscoll. Mr. Lockyer?"

James Lockyer was powerful in his speech. He outlined the history of the case to the court. He then summarized the evidence. He went on to say,

> *Tammy, despite all of this, always maintained her innocence. Her prison records show the way she stuck up for herself. The response of the prison psychologist . . . was that the reason she was denying having murdered her son was because she was suffering from amnesia. She came to AIDWYC in the late 1990s and asked for our help. And then . . . in 2005, it was finally realized, really a decade later . . . that Dr. Smith was really something of a charlatan in his business.*

James Lockyer looked at the small figure of Tammy on the bench. She sat there plainly shaken and sobbing as he told of the events since 1993. "I think it is only right that I, in a sense, let Tammy have the last word through her affidavit filed in the Court of Appeal. Her life for so many years has been an enormous tragedy. But there is some good news that we can end up with. It's contained there in her affidavit, right at the end." He read out aloud for the court.

*"On September 8th of 2010, I gave birth to a
daughter whom Rick"* — her husband — *"and
I named Tiffany. Tiffany is living with Rick's
mother in Toronto . . . we plan to move in with
her later this month."* And indeed, they did.
*"Tiffany is doing well and I continue to take
counselling"* — and I am adding a bit here to
the affidavit — *through the bail program at the
Canterbury House in Toronto.* "*I did not cause
Kenneth's death. I loved him like any mother
loves her child. I would never have intentionally
harmed him. I think about him every day and
wish I could have him back. I miss my two other
sons who were taken from me so early in their
lives."* But to finish, despite what she has been
through, she's a strong lady . . . I think, speaking as a human being rather than as a counsel,
that she really does have some very good hopes
in her future. Thank you, Your Honour.

Now it was Justice Brown's turn to speak. "Thank
you very much, Mr. Lockyer. Ms. Marquardt, the murder
charge against you has been withdrawn at the request of
the Crown. Before these proceedings come to a close, I
would like to say a few brief comments to you."

This was a very moving time for Tammy. For fourteen years, she had been looking forward to hearing this. The judge went on,

Justice Goudge in his report on the Inquiry into Paediatric Forensic Pathology said that the sudden, unexpected death of a child is a devastating event for parents, for family, and for the entire community . . . and I know that was certainly the case for you . . . the failed pathology of Dr. Charles Smith has had a traumatic impact on your life as well as that of your family and friends . . . I can't imagine what it must have been like for you to have had to bear the burden of not only losing your child Kenneth, but also to have had to deal with the fact that you were accused of killing your son, convicted for that alleged crime, and also spent thirteen years in jail as a result. In addition, your sons Keith and Eric were also taken from you so early in their lives . . .

Ms. Marquardt, nothing I can say to you today will repair the damage that has been caused to you . . . nothing I can say today can bring back your son Kenneth, for whom I know you still

grieve. I wish my words today could do that. As the Court of Appeal for Ontario acknowledged in its judgment of April 8, 2011, your conviction in this case constituted a miscarriage of justice. I appreciate that my words today may seem inadequate. But I offer to you, Ms. Marquardt, my deepest expression of regret that you had to endure all that you have endured as a result of miscarriage of justice in this case. It is my fervent hope that somehow you are able to start to pick up the pieces of your life again and to begin to live your life outside the shadow of a criminal prosecution. The Crown's withdrawal of the murder charge today brings an end to these criminal proceedings and any bail restrictions that accompany that charge.

I wish you the very best of luck as you embark on this new phase of your life, free of the restrictions the criminal justice system has placed upon you since your arrest in 1993. You're free to go ma'am. Thank you.

Tammy cried. She was shaking in her chair. *Finally, finally they accept my innocence.* James Lockyer let her cry the tears of the years lost. She sobbed for the children lost and the life lost. She sobbed for every tragedy that had beset her life. If only tears could wash away those memories.

17

CHAPTER SEVENTEEN

THE OPEN WOUNDS OF LOSS

"DEATH IS NOT THE GREATEST LOSS IN LIFE.
THE GREATEST LOSS IS WHAT DIES INSIDE US
WHILE WE LIVE."

— NORMAN COUSINS

Tammy stepped out into the sunshine a free woman. She was free of the burden of shame. Free of the accusations against her. The press and media stormed her

"I'm free. I am free," she said, in a voice filled with emotion. She displayed the tattoo — an eagle with the word "freedom" inked into her skinny arm.

"Honestly, I never thought I would see this day. I thought there is no justice. They are going to believe him [Smith] and they're not going to believe someone like me."

Tammy squinted in the bright sunshine in her

pixie-cropped hair and blue dress. She held up a photo of Kenneth. "Well, all these years I do not think Kenneth has been able to rest in peace because of everything that's been going on. Now he is finally able to be at rest. It's been too long."

Somewhere in the crowd a reporter asked, "How about the two boys who were taken away from you?"

"I hope that one day they will agree to come and see me. Hopefully, they will be told after today that they were adopted and who I am . . . that way they will be aware and come to find me. And I will be there for them. They are teenagers now and I do not want to disturb their lives." Tammy had placed her name on a registry so that they could find her.

Another reporter asked, "What would you say to Dr. Charles Smith if you met up with him?"

"I cannot say this on TV." She smiled, paused, and then went on, "I will ask him 'Why? What possessed you to play God?'"

Though she was brief on this point outside the court-house, Tammy had provided an Impact Statement at the request of the Discipline Committee of the College of Physicians and Surgeons of Ontario (CPSO). It expressed the impact that Dr. Charles Smith's testimony had on her life. Her statement was addressed to him:

To be accused and convicted of the murder of Kenneth was the beginning of my nightmare. A nightmare that just got worse and seemingly unending as I entered into the harsh and unnerving Canadian penal system. Prison became my reality for the next thirteen years. I woke up each day to prison's unpredictable craziness. I endured the taunting, name calling, and death threats. I went to bed each night wondering whether my two sons were in good and loving homes. Were they healthy, happy, and doing well in school? I starved for news of them. But none came. And so, when I wasn't dealing with the cold dankness and inhumanity of prison, I hoped that someone, anyone, would believe me and that I would be exonerated and freed. I prayed. Oh how I prayed that I would be granted one more miracle; being reunited with my boys. I have suffered from deep bouts of depression, anger, bitterness. I often wondered if I would ever be able to find the joy and laughter I once knew as a young mother.

The heartbreak and pain of losing Kenneth was unimaginable. But to be declared his murderer

*has unrelentingly tortured my mind and the
depths of my soul.*

*The truth didn't seem to matter. Even my own
family chose to believe your expert opinion.*

*There is nothing that can be done to erase the
horror of losing a child and years of imprisonment. I wish there was. I wish an apology from
you would be the magical cure. But although it
would be comforting to know that you are sorry
for the devastation you have caused, it would
not and could not stop the longing for the return
of Kenneth and his two brothers.*

This is a story of loss. Tammy lost her two sons Keith
and Eric who were adopted out. In turn, they lost their
birth mother. Tammy lost her freedom. She lost the
opportunity to be happy, bond with her family, and live
her life. Tammy's wrongful conviction caused her great
humiliation and disgrace. She was physically assaulted in
prison. She was always in danger from the inmates who
thought she had killed her son.

She lost her belief in the justice system, the police,
the state, and society. Tammy's physical and psychological

well-being was greatly affected. She has ongoing hospital, medical, and psychological treatment expenses for emotional distress and post-traumatic stress disorder.

The public's faith in the medical profession, the justice system, and the state was also shaken. In 2009, the Ontario government announced compensation for families affected by wrongful convictions caused by Dr. Charles Smith. Individuals could claim up to $250,000 each. A child of someone wrongly accused who had been removed from the family home could claim up to $25,000. A family member directly affected by a relative's conviction could claim up to $12,500. Legal costs incurred by the wrongly accused would also be paid. In June 2011, PostMedia reported that the government paid out $5.5 million to the victims of Dr. Smith's flawed testimonies.

The Goudge inquiry cost over $9.4 million. For all that she went through, Tammy received $250,000 from the government of Ontario.

Since being charged on November 23, 1993, Tammy spent thirteen years and eight months in prison. She spent more than four years on bail under strict rules. At last she was a free woman. In December 2011, Tammy met her sons Keith (age sixteen) and Eric (age fifteen).

She has tried to move forward. She still faces the tests of addictions. Because of all she suffered, she is suing

Charles Smith, the Hospital for Sick Children, James Young and James Cairns (both in the OCCO at that time), and the province of Ontario. The civil case was filed in the Ontario Superior Court of Justice.

Tammy claimed total damages of $13 million. At the time this is being written, she awaits the results of this civil suit. In the meantime, she is trying to pick up the threads of her life and move on. She visits Kenneth's grave often. Tammy hopes that somewhere he is at peace. Somewhere from beyond, Kenneth calls to her.

Don't cry for me my mother
I know how much you care
I know you tried to help me
And how hard it is to bear.

Don't cry for me my mother
Wipe the creases from your brow
I stand beside you every hour
You are out of prison now.

Don't cry for me my mother
Let not your trials be in vain
I'm happy on the other side
Free of all the pain.

AUTHOR'S NOTE

In the writing of this book, I have used official documents, media reports, blogs, the Association in Defence of the Wrongly Convicted (AIDWYC) website, the Goudge inquiry reports, academic articles on wrongful convictions, and media interviews with Tammy Marquardt. In the narrative construction of her feelings, I used some latitude to build on the various expressions she made about her feelings to reporters and other interviewers or in affidavits and transcripts in court.

Some of the dialogue is constructed from the court documents in the public domain, but the punctuation has been slightly modified without changing the essence, to enable easy reading. Some of the dialogues have also been simplified for the same purpose.

TIMELINE

OCTOBER 9, 1993, 4:38 P.M.: Tammy discovers Kenneth in bed, entangled in the sheets. She calls 911.

OCTOBER 12, 1993: Kenneth is declared brain dead and is taken off life support systems.

OCTOBER 21, 1993: Tammy goes to a bar and gets drunk. She screams repeatedly that she killed Kenneth, because she forgot how to give him CPR.

NOVEMBER 23, 1993: Tammy Marquardt is charged with the murder of her son Kenneth and arrested. She is later released on bail pending her trial.

AUGUST 17, 1994: Tammy gives birth to Rick Marquardt's son, Keith. Keith was taken away from her by the CAS.

FALL 1995: Tammy's case comes up for trial. Before the trial, the Crown prosecutor offers her a five-year plea bargain. Tammy turns it down, insisting she is innocent.

OCTOBER 24, 1995: Tammy is convicted of second-degree murder in the death of her son Kenneth.

DECEMBER 7, 1995: Tammy is sentenced to life imprisonment without eligibility for parole for ten years. She is taken to Prison for Women, Kingston, to serve her sentence.

JUNE 20, 1996: Tammy gives birth to Eric at the

Kingston General Hospital.

JUNE 21, 1996: Eric is taken away from her.

SPRING 1997: Tammy is transferred to Grand Valley Institution, Kitchener, Ontario.

JANUARY 16, 1998: Tammy's appeal comes up for hearing.

JANUARY 22, 1998: Tammy's appeal is dismissed.

JULY 1998: Tammy attempts to take her life with a large quantity of Tylenol and other assorted pills. After recuperating for three days in hospital, she is transferred back to Prison for Women, Kingston.

APRIL 2000: The Prison for Women, Kingston, is shut down and Tammy is transferred to the Grand Valley Institution, Kitchener, once again.

2001: Tammy gets approval to have temporary absences to the local epilepsy society. Her security classification is changed from medium to minimum.

2002: Three complaints to the College of Physicians and Surgeons of Ontario (CPSO) relating to Dr. Charles Smith's work in suspicious death cases are upheld.

MARCH 2004: The parole board approves Tammy's entry into a year-long program, during which she is allowed regular but supervised visits to the Elizabeth Fry Society in Toronto.

EARLY   2004:   Tammy seeks the assistance of AIDWYC. They assign David Bayliss to the case.

APRIL 2005: AIDWYC writes to Dr. Barry McLellan and the attorney general of Ontario to request a full public inquiry into Dr. Charles Smith's work.

JUNE   2005:   Tammy gets her first unescorted temporary absence pass to go to the Elizabeth Fry Society in Toronto.

JUNE 7, 2005: Dr. Barry McLellan announces the Chief Coroner's Review on Dr. Charles Smith's work.

NOVEMBER 1, 2005: Dr. McLellan announces that the Office of the Chief Coroner had selected forty-four cases of Dr. Charles Smith and also provided the names of four external pathologists who would form the review panel.

FALL   2006:   Tammy's parole is suspended after she tests positive for cocaine. She gets parole again a few weeks later.

APRIL   2007:   Tammy's parole is suspended again when she tests positive for cocaine. A month later, she is out again.

APRIL 19, 2007: Dr. Barry McLellan releases his report on the Chief Coroner's Review.

APRIL 25, 2007: The Government of Ontario establishes the Inquiry into Paediatric Forensic

Pathology in Ontario, under the Public Inquiries Act (better known as the Goudge inquiry).

AUGUST 2007: Tammy's parole is suspended once again.

NOVEMBER 30, 2007: Tammy's parole is revoked due to her inability to cope with the outside world.

OCTOBER 2007: Dr. Saukko, who was appointed by the Goudge inquiry, presents a full medically legal report on Kenneth's death, stating that determination on the cause of death was "in error."

FEBRUARY 10, 2009: Tammy applies to the Supreme Court of Canada seeking leave to appeal along with an application for an extension of time.

FEBRUARY 11, 2009: Tammy is granted an extension of time to seek leave to appeal.

MARCH 12, 2009: Tammy is released on bail.

APRIL 30, 2009: Tammy's case is remanded to the Court of Appeal for Ontario for consideration of fresh evidence and whether Tammy's conviction constitutes a miscarriage of justice.

SEPTEMBER 8, 2010: Tammy gives birth to a daughter, Tiffany.

FEBRUARY 1, 2011: Dr. Charles Smith's certificate of registration is revoked and he is directed to pay costs of $3,650.

FEBRUARY 10, 2011: Tammy's appeal comes up for hearing and her conviction is construed as a miscarriage of justice.

JUNE 7, 2011: Tammy's case comes before court as a result of the Court of Appeal setting aside the conviction for second-degree murder and ordering a new trial. The Crown withdraws the charge against Tammy and she is declared a free woman.

DECEMBER 2011: Tammy is reunited with her sons Keith and Eric.

JANUARY 11, 2013: Tammy files a civil suit against Dr. Charles Smith, The Hospital for Sick Children, James Young, James Cairns, and Her Majesty the Queen in the Right of Ontario.

GLOSSARY

ACQUITTAL: the verdict when someone accused of a crime is found not guilty, or there is a lack of evidence, or when guilt is not proven beyond a reasonable doubt.

AIDWYC: Association in Defence of the Wrongly Convicted

APPEAL: a request to review a case that has already been decided in court.

ASPHYXIA: When the body is deprived of oxygen, usually caused by smothering or strangulation.

AUTOPSY: a specialized surgical procedure that examines a corpse to determine the cause and manner of death. It may also be done to examine the presence of disease or injury and its effects on the organs of the body.

CAS: Children's Aid Society

CONVICTION: the verdict when someone accused of a crime is found guilty.

CPR: Cardiopulmonary resuscitation

CPSO: College of Physicians and Surgeons of Ontario

CROWN PROSECUTOR: the lawyer(s) acting for the government, or "the Crown," in court proceedings. They are the prosecutors in Canada's legal system.

DEMEANOUR: A person's outward actions or behaviour.

EPILEPSY: a medical disorder involving episodes of abnormal electrical discharge in the brain.

FORENSICS: the study of medical facts in relation to legal cases.

JURY: a criminal trial is decided by a group of twelve randomly selected citizens from the province in which the trial is held. All twelve must agree on a verdict.

MANSLAUGHTER: the unlawful killing of a human being without malice or forethought.

OCCO: Office of the Chief Coroner for Ontario

OPFPU: Ontario Paediatric Forensic Pathology Unit

PATHOLOGIST: a doctor who studies diseases and illnesses by examining matter such as organs, tissues, cells, and fluids. They also examine biopsy material and provide a diagnosis on such analysis.

PAROLE: the supervised release from prison to the community before the full sentence has been served. A prisoner on parole must agree to certain restrictions and report regularly to a parole officer.

PAEDIATRIC: the area of medicine deading with the care of children and infants.

SHAKEN BABY SYNDROME: child abuse caused by intentional shaking.

SUDEP: Sudden and Unexpected Death in Epilepsy

TESTIMONY: the statement of a witness under oath.

VERDICT: the decision of the jury at the end of a trial, usually guilty or not guilty.

FURTHER READING

TAMMY'S 1998 APPEAL:
http://caselaw.canada.globe24h.com/0/0/ontario/
court-of-appeal-for-ontario/1998/01/22/r-v-mar-
quardt-1998-3527-on-ca.shtml.

THE GOUDGE INQUIRY REPORT:
http://www.attorneygeneral.jus.gov.on.ca/inquiries/
goudge/report/.

WRONGFUL CONVICTIONS:
James Lockyer, "Forensic Pediatric Pathology and
Wrongful Convictions," March 29, 2012. https://www.
nacdl.org/uploadedFiles/files/resource_center/topics/
post_conviction/02_Pediatric_Pathology_Materials.pdf.

Kent Roach, "Wrongful Convictions in Canada,"
University of Cincinnati Law Review, Volume 80, Issue 4,
Article 19, 9-8-2013.

ACKNOWLEDGEMENTS

In the making of this book, so many people have helped me directly and indirectly. For putting me in touch with Tammy's lawyers, acquiring photographs, and lending me her own photography appearing in this book, I am deeply grateful to Win Wahrer, Client Director of AIDWYC.

Joe Shapiro from NPR, Washington, lent me photographs and spoke to me on the phone about his own impressions of Tammy and his interview with her. For this I am very grateful.

To Pam Hickman, my editor, who did what editors do — enhance the quality of the book — I am very grateful. She was most graceful and respectful, and it was such a pleasure to work with her.

Many thanks to Catherine Dorton for her copy-editing of the book and the many others who worked to refine this work.

I thank the publisher, James Lorimer, for this commission, and I enjoyed working with his publishing house.

Willy Vestering, for your generosity in meeting me, talking about Prison for Women, and providing me the photographs of the prison, I thank you.

Carolyn and Peter McCarney, for your help in setting me on this path, I remember you fondly and with gratitude.

Clarke Mackey, thank you for sending me your documentary on Prison for Women and putting me in touch with Willy.

Dr. Rosemary Meier, thank you for putting me in touch with Win.

To Artscape Gibraltar Point, the artist residence on Toronto islands, thank you for the residency that allowed me the space to write and interact with so many talented artists.

Fr. Kozar, thank you for the numerous ways you have helped me.

To Philomena Saldanha, Melwyn D'Costa, Dionne D'Costa, Kiev and Kian D'Costa, with whom I spent my homeless days as I was writing this book, I am eternally grateful.

To the Ontario Arts Council for the grant in writing this book, my grateful thanks.

INDEX